Melancholy Maelstrom

A DIARY OF SILVER LININGS

Damilare Yusuff

MELANCHOLY MAELSTROM

A Diary of Silver Linings

Content

Mantra

I am whatever I say I am

If I wasn't then why would I say I am

Everyday I invoke the will of man

There is no other way I am

\- Damilare

Damilare Yusuff

Introduction

This book was an exorcism for me. I wrote it during time of despair and facing my own mortality. Where I didn't know what time I would feel okay. Each poem and each essay, including this introduction was written in pain, early mornings, during a shock, or late evening. Many days spent in my room quietly contemplating my existence, waking up in cold sweats all of this during the end of 2018 and early of 2019.

Before I even decided I was going to publish these in a book, this was a release an escape from the world outside my body. Away from something that would give me pain or have me feel less than; where I nursed the emotions of anger and wrath from betrayal and condescension of a system that is supposedly made to help.

These works pulled negativity from my spirit, collected away and cleaned in the ocean of my mind because these thoughts were not allowed right to stay they were just passing through. My 2019 had no place for negativity, my

2019 should be good, full of forward movement and growth. Anything else may pass through but cannot stay.

My desire to make a book has always been high I did not see this being my first, this was very necessary for my growth. Someone told me the content had value and something told me to give it to whoever needs it.

This book is and always will be about the art, I gave into myself and allowed the gift to work through me and with that the poetry came freely as a reward. I spent months just speaking in the code of my poetry and till I wrote it down there was no part of me that would let it go.

That has been the main drive these past months to just let go and release all the things that were holding me back as if this was spiritual passage or awakening to better artistry, like I said I don't know what will come from this on the readers side but on my side this is freedom.

The storms my spirit has had to endure and live through are truly *that which would kill me*, my pain. Sickle Cell didn't bring the poetry, my fear of the hospital and crippling anxiety I get from mediocre doctors bought about these essays with rhythm. The shame they try to make feel, the undermining tone and demeaning attitude, the not so subtle cockiness with the words they use all in say, 'I am a doctor you should listen to me I know better than you. I AM better than you.'

So if you enjoyed this work thank all the doctors in the UK and rest of the world that half ass patient care and Google the things they don't fully understand… Those among us that live in a virtual critical condition of an invisible disease bear the brunt of it, we are the testing ground for these doctors everywhere.

Thank them for me, - revere the look in their eyes as they watch the clock biding their time as they wait till their shift ends. The times I've been in the Hospital and the look in their eyes fully expose their lustre for helping people is non existent - I know my demons do.

The moment I lived this out in the face of those that are there to take names blood and pressure I feel the behemoth slowly pressing down on my chest the corners of the room fade the people turn into an audience for my potential breakdown and as I have less than my natural proficiency to help people to help myself and my art supplies are sitting sound at home, the shaking of my hands turned to typing and those words to poetry.

I never asked for this, I asked for a normal life. We don't always get what we asked for, There are things in life that just happen, I got no more than I could handle, my experiences have shown me my depth. Living now and being able to share is allowing a release of the pressure of that behemoth and the blowing of my sail altering my course away from the Storms of existence. This is the passage to an equilibrium, freedom hasn't shown its face to me but, this brief therapeutic release is an empathetic plea and partly an education in a form I am able to share in without fear.

Damilare Yusuff

1

There's a big part of my life where I have been made to just suffer through moments, episodes and crisis with painkillers. When I was younger we some how managed to keep it all in-house, work together and there was no part of my days spent in hospital which is amazingly uncharacteristic of someone in my condition, love got me through most things.

How 'Share For Self Care' came about was me understanding In the words of people around me my terrible life – but I will always attribute it to the unbearable anxiety I suffered for the very first time in A&E where writing was my only release and solace. It wasn't just I decided to write poetry I need to write poetry these poems just happened through a time I was suffering mentally & physically and no one was around to understand me or my feelings, so instead of acting out my pain, I would write it down.

Share for self care is a multilayered not just from the emotional side, where everything is dark & you separate yourself because 'I am not my pain' but the process of sharing good and bad can be cathartic for the person talking and listening and there's a way both can engage the other better.

Sharing hasn't been difficult for me and until recently neither has articulation. What Made this was the communication of how i feel to better improve someone else's understanding of my feelings and I gather it is amazing to give.

Share For Self Care

I want to explain this concept of self care, through sharing.

There's this thing that happens when you share without fearing -

Your mind is open and the pistons start firing

The hate is silenced by harmony of the engine in your mind, it's inspiring.

There is something you're able to hear — it's that one person that would be part of your positivity

What you did was add to their life what they lacked and they want to say it to you clear, you invited creativity,

I know self hate runs deep but the love is the clear sky of the day that your mind all day round.

Love runs loud because the care is a cycle it's clean, unsullied, and fills the air with floral sweet smells as your mind runs through the meadow of the summers day and now you're acquainted with your positive influence again.

You share for your self and it takes care of others, till you do it you won't know that was the exchange you made invited the love into the life you live.

Mind is filled with so much static, so messy but love makes it tranquil you want everyone to feel the pleasures of the freedom that love gives.

Sharing it feels good, it frees the mind as long as the intention is pure and true the equivalent exchange will be valuable.

You can't ask for someone to give you peace of mind because you're sharing something that will disrupt their peace of mind, even I would give you a piece of my mind. Stay conscious of your words that expose a truth that doesn't express the spirit of love remember how it felt in the beginning you gave them a piece of your heart a heap of emotion the hope that someone would feel it in a good way & hope they'd share it with another person. That's the version of love we share that overlaps with self care.

2

The writing of 'Tell Him, Take It All' was one of the final days of my tumultuous journey, I spent time wallowing, living in my pain my only respite being able to write it down. This bought out a fire in me and poetry I accept.

I have to admit I enjoyed writing, although it was my pain it felt like I was stripping myself from the symbiosis syndrome —I hate Sickle Cell so I also hate myself.— Some people suffer from not just Sickle Cell pain, Our minds will make us think we are our pain. I am of the mind pain is just a thing that happens, breaking that bondage between who you are and the pain that rift empowered me and I'm sure it can empower you. This goes for all pain in all forms.

'Tell Him, Take it All' was a time where I felt like I was being uplifted by a higher power and partly the reason I wrote this book, as an exchange of ideas and as a way to always remember that.

Just because it happened to me once doesn't mean it doesn't happen all the time; and the power to get over and deal with my pain in a healthy way is a blessing so I have to say Alhamdulillah at least once here to pay respects.

Tell Him, Take It All

Tell him he can take it all. My pain my fears, my agony my despair and tears.

Culture my mind and I will cultivate the fruit the soil bears for us to reap together and share so those around can see their own seed and take care. Of their spirits too, you can clear your mind or fill it with goo, that sticky slimy sludge holding the same influence as daily to a slug.

Formed from years of having none but now your spirits one filled the cracks of the baron land with tears that stream through the channels like a baby in their mother's hands - I feel free in the mother land.

Told him take it all now I can see past the tempest the storm has cleared the time has passed he took my spirit higher same as the way the floods raised Noah's ark. Hark - - - the heart I have is for those that are free from the bondage of holding onto the dam that is keeping your emotions pressurised, slow release or let it ALL go and he'll take it FOR SURE, trust him. Ask your mother, it's okay. She'll hold and guide you, through you as your spirit is holding on to the emotions congruent in holding in freedom. With the open arms that is a complete man who successfully let go has fulfilled the path, you trusted and he become a conduit to let you in the kingdom. His peace is mine, it can be us all ask him- take it, I'm sure he'll bear it all.

I cannot talk about this as if it's a casual matter. Tell him take it all, was also written as a prayer because when someone out here makes you feel shame for who you may be you can grow resentful of that person or thing. So Tell Him Take It All

3

Many patients of Sickle Cell go through trauma and suffering by the hands of people who think they're addicts or believe them to be in less pain than they actually are, this is well studied and documented discrimination, partly by race and also lack of understanding of Sickle Cell. I take to this matter with diligence and empathy and a serious intensity of someone with a mission. It wasn't just a stress relief, I found out facts that scared me; the best way to get the point across is through story.

I was talking to someone that also has Sickle Cell and we got in a deep debate about opioids, how Sickle Cell patients are reliant on them and how painkillers help numb the mind to the pain but doesn't get rid of pain by any stretch of the imagination. Our conversation came at a paradigm shifting highway when they told me 'I don't want to be going to a dealer buying weed', They had the thought of looking like an addict. I told them for what its worth you go to your doctors every couple months for opioids, the doctors are our proverbial dealer.

Whatever frame of mind they had after that was shattered because we're not in a place to judge what people do to treat their condition and going to the doctor for drugs doesn't make it any more right when treating our condition considering we can only positively remove the pain for now.

Recently I've been asking why do we get an ailment for our pain but not a treatment for the cause these questions aren't answered by the doctors and medical industry that has been treating this condition for almost a century now, they prefer the lull of pushing off the condition to just pain factors and not the real affliction of low blood movement.

The real deal is this is a very early time in the treatment of Sickle Cell and for the most part we're stuck in the 70's with our cultural understanding, people have no positive image of those with sickle cell nor do they feel to bother with dealing with it openly. The culture is very much a 'keep it to yourself' one till its pertinent to talk about it.

The whole ordeal seems contrived because all doctors give us to affect Sickle Cell is Pain Killers, while treating us like addicts when we ask for them because Sickle Cell is not a strong part of the curriculum. I've been told Doctors get a 30 minute segment of a lecture on Sickle Cell on a whole Hematology curriculum. This brings about strong feelings within me and I cant help but write a works on it, which is a reason I started *Sickle Cell Companion.*

My Power is Greater than Addiction

Coffee in my cup is full

And so is the dose of my opioids too

Save myself from feeling green

But cloud my mind from what is true

 I cannot be addicted to what I don't enjoy,

All I know is I fear pain more than highs.

I can do what my doctor prescribed ,

Or I can suffer in silence and muffle internal cries.

Sometimes I feel there's only two options

Feel pain or feel highs

But I opt for a third function

Fight the pain without a disguise

Fight so my body is stronger

Be the warrior I'm supposed to emulate

Fight so pain and highs aren't the only answer

Be the man who was made to create

Create the third option and become a key

For my brothers and sisters for them not to plead,

For drugs, as they never wanted any

Retract the power from pharmaceutical greed

4

It is well known Sickle Cell Patients are not prone to get addicted to opioids so people thinking such helps us further understand the lack of literature that is actually consumed. I'm noticing there is more care for treatment of symptoms than treatment of the actual cause of the pain

I will be using my power to manifest a positive change. We must look after our bodies & not fall into the downwards spiral of symbiotic self hate causing further mental & spiritual stress, causing us to fall far into depravity.

I wanted to share and be open sharing of this book my determination to help my brothers and sisters. It hasn't always been that way I haven't always had the energy to at fight at 100% sometimes I get tired and life want to just do its thing at the end of the day I love myself through-and-through.

There have been many accounts to point to where I was racially discriminated against and some of them defined my life during a time where my pain was attacking me the worst during my life. It's not easy to do what I did and bring this type of mentality forward, I understand that. I thank God for all the power he's granted me.

I Love Myself

I've noticed the love for my self is true. The way I never finished that boy in school

That called me nigger thought it was cool,

What's the point if clapping brothers heads together when people applaud the braggadocios fool

So comfortable in his ignorance like a stooge

Still I shook his hand and we started anew

It was only the love of myself that saved them from my wrath,

The wrath of a changing tide that I was in no control of almost made me lose my path

Sweeping me off my feet having me lose composure.

You know like limestone over time the acid rains would cause erosion

Imagine, Two weeks in my they called me nigger,

That shit is traumatising at least they'd have you figure.

This is what my time in this hell hole will be like, me a real G. being taken down by the system?

Teacher holding me back the Isle I see making me think I'm not good enough to be great, they really tried to break me... got me good... even got me wanting to end it all on most days... Or pay them back in the worst way... I could feel the psyche up in my gut

What's the point if I don't love myself enough to tell me what they said isn't true. It's NOT.

So the love I have for myself must be true cos, although De-bbish made it seem like the higher range wasn't in my reach - me aiming for the top-shelf,

She was the lighthouse ("she thought") on shore who told me my ship wasn't going to make the tide, the low-c mark would crush me, - from the ground up.- Seemed to be their aim but it wasn't mine I live in true distinction my level of prognosis for my firm conditions were higher.

Though, there was cause for disruption this rocks tried to stick me, that year it was sticky but what set me apart was my critics. This ship wasn't sinking I made it to shore I built the Trophaeum bigger than the lighthouse to adorn my win of the time told the story more times an even more important I named it Titan. I showed them I love myself, I love this work too nothing can keep me from the path that I'm reaching.

So my love has got to be true what else cold keep me fighting for years suffering alone in hospital crying for the pain to go away

Mac in front of me like I'm an MUA, — every time the pain became sufferable I continued to work but I knew this couldn't last forever I had to put a stop to the pain that I felt no one should live like this not even my worst enemy could live through the shit I been through.

Not without love. They say anything is possible but I make the improbable possible spirit of a warrior ask my dad he has the stories of which my ancestors built from. Fellow warriors died while I survived all the near death experiences waking up to the reaper at the foot of my bed. What pulled me out of the dark life was love. I have to tell you. If I didn't love myself I wouldn't have this point of view. Sometimes the fight is too much, the life gets enough. More morphine in my veins than fluid it's impossible to imagine what kept me going all this time. Lived nary a day without peace of mind. It's love

5

Love took me through seeing my course mates graduate of course I would celebrate I'm not a loser who could touch me no one else was there while I was squeezing on the pump like asthma compressions. Wish I could breath maybe I should ask the fluid in my lungs. I made sure anything is possible with my mind and my will I made sure every fight with the reaper and my spirit didn't kill.

Kept my mind in books continued learning only solace in the suffering was the fulfilling the task of my spirit to my mind to make me a formidable force and anyone or any thing would hear the song my spirit sings. Who killed the reaper? Surely not me I am my brothers keeper is he that to me? That's a poem for another day this one is for the love of me. I love my soul I love myself because if I didn't other souls would cry as well for a brother gone before his time because he wanted to die and not live through this hell.

I looked back at those time at my white school and the racist pupils and head of year and in college again and my times in the hospital where I almost died put them side by side and measured them. There's multiple ways to kill a man, I was at points where it was either the people or 'myself, I felt I was the Sickle Cell pain at this point; the pain that was made to kill me but I didn't die. There are lonely nights and mornings in hospitals where I cried but I never died, what was the point? 'There's more life to live' I kept telling myself.

Bringing me to the point where I thought - if I am going to die I would have as much fun as possible. - What was fun then? I had no idea I lived by plans and strategy and at 20 I plotted to change the course of my life which I effectively did because I didn't face not one thing head on I was a man dealing with trauma in boyish ways. It's not a way to live but my life wasn't planned past 22 I expected nothing more from my teenage mind.

When a young man first knows how to earn money in abundance the only thing he know to do with it is blow it; that's exactly what happened to me , at 22 I didn't learn to be frugal because that's not my personality type. I learned to pay my future self & spend in the future, and have fun with what's left at 25 I learned to pay back in installments because that's a better strategy than paying a whole. Like many things in life this lesson was hard taught, I vowed to never be broke like then again.

Parched at sea - Dying of Thirst

The days I never have to worry what I'd have to eat that day, this isn't really Remembrance Sunday and those aren't my brothers no MORE,

I wiped the scoreboard clean and said I don't want to compete ANYMORE.

Everything used to be for a score, things I killed that day I'm eating now.

Because whatever I spend I can make it back tomorrow.

I'm more about cultivating life and saving it for winter time.

But there's nothing to save on this rainy summer day & every thing I killed I ate that day it was mine,

And didn't save for a rainy day I didn't build for the time to LAST, my life was too cheap back then I was living fast.

The habits I had back then they didn't die just as quick,

And upon my declaration my karmic clock started to tick.

Light his shit up set it ablaze, treat life like a Viking. When the body is spent push it out to sea light a bon fire and party that day.

For me that was typical cos that's the competing way.

All the spending, drunken Lying, caught up with me I was too stupid to understand that a mans cultivates the ground he conquers, instead of piss it away.

— And all the cheers are traded with debt letters for all them bodies there's a price to pay.

So now I'm dying of thirst, the only thing that comes round every once in a while is a buzzard waiting to see my time is done,

But the only thing it sees is the end of my gun.

The land is barren my barrel is stocked,

— Buzzards are cheap and the time I spent in this famine fortified my spirit so empty it is not

What I did was stayed still waited patient,

Sleeping in a foetal position I know I'm prepared and they're preparing for my fall for me to come on my hands and knees to beg and pray so I can eat and survive to the next day, continue on my path recycling the same food; eating the same fish; sitting on this boat during summer thinking of the same shit; the things I think about is gracious.

The day I talk about my story and all the things I've been through, keeping it light-hearted because if they really knew what I been through they would really cry like they're beside me right there on that make shift bed that same make shift pillow wondering how I put myself back together.

I wasn't so broke as my soul was whole you could tell me my funds were - whatever.

No one can tell me my spirit is cheap today as I said I Cultivate. There one solid theme throughout the competing -

— I would always celebrate when my friends was eating. -

— They may not have shared they didn't come from the same philosophy as me, so I will never blame someone for that.

I was a killer whale in the zoo feeding on guppies, now I'm a killer whale playing free in the wild feasting — on sharks.

And what would set me apart from the sharks is that I'm still splitting with my brothers break down half a half and share it with them since they didn't share, as I said I still share with my brothers just to know I am fair.

Damilare Yusuff

6

For one reason or the other I've always liked the ocean. Distinguished, well known, feared, desired & still working on discovering what is in it all. Much like my mind and the lessons I've been taught whether that be self hate or my physical limiter and mental blocks stopping me from giving my all in certain regards because I'm scared to get hurt.

The ocean reminds me of a story I wrote in university about a small boy called Frederick, who bugged his father and mother day after day to take him to the beach. Even painting a mural on his wall after that, one qualifying day they obliged. Frederick ran from the car to the beach side and looked out to the vastness, wondering if there was an edge.

Leaving his parents behind on the sand he went to a cliff to get a greater vantage point and with no hesitation jumped in - to the dismay of his parents - while under water he swore he saw flashing colour and lights and insisted he got swallowed by a whale. Being washed up by the shore he would go home and paint over the mural and was happy with the result.

Damilare Yusuff

If you understood that short story then well done.

A Storm is a Coming

I speak a lot about a storm the spirit and titans. Waves whirlpools and maelstrom because I discovered my mind was like an ocean, it was designed to be vast and forever moving with intent like the sharks and the dolphins. There's so much to map I can keep finding shit, what I discovered at last there's no end to it.

The human mind is much bigger than the body, what you put in is what you get out much like the killer whales that are predators that will knock a shark out. Circle of life down there is like an idea up here the bigger ideas eat the smaller ones but the meanest ones will pierce your lungs have you out of breath drowning in your own fears because what you put in is what you get out and those ones end in tears. Now you're choking and can't breath much coughing and wheezing make you throw up your steamed lunch, killing you softly making it a long year.

There's a storm in your mind and you're alarmed but no one cares Cos the can't see your fear, you hide from it again and again but it creeps up, bite you like a shark rip your spleen up but you don't need that so you carry on till your gall bladder fucks up leave you with kidney stones.

See Your body it speaks to you but your mind is the puppeteer pulling the string have you distracted from the real fears, and you wonder why you have a long year. Till the storm creeps up again lighting strikes you but you never know till the thunder hit you on your body like a Charlie Watts.

Remember I said you get in what you get out. This is the thing instead of being captain of your ship you play the first mate. I never let life happens guide the ship and eat my blues like the Japanese do. I never started poetry for no reason this what I'm meant to do, my blues are long and they forever happened. But I worked it out on my craft put the work in me so that will never happen. I mean life, it won't happen to me I cut past my storms never let them happen to me. See a maelstrom coming I thought I might lose my life, but kept my mettle heavy, stood firm at the helm like a preacher at the pulpit, I'm the master not the puppet - so I cut my strings. I rode the lighting surfed the wave, the fears said Kill 'em all louder than Lars Ulric on stage.

I'm not telling you I've got no storms I'm telling you I've lived through them all. I've managed the falls and I've starved through winters ration my food and always gave half to my brothers, on the other side of the storms, there's sharing and everything I've been through I'm sharing because self care let's you survive the big fears. I've cried too, keep telling people I've almost died too, but there's no glorifying that so you make a metaphor; about a storm; paint a picture in your readers mind; probably sing it on stage; for them to scream encore.

7

We all have our storms and ways of getting through them, I learned how to spot mine, which earned me the ability to spot others'. I use caution to not slip into a flow of destructive bad habits that also lead to downwards spirals into the depths of turmoil and terror carefully navigate them. It's easier said than done, but this is why as a youngster I was devoted to learning my bodies and it's triggers so I never have to use pain killers as often.

If one of those time come I know how to handle it, it's the life that was chosen from me and I have to choose not to be defined by it and consequently I define myself and No one else

If one of those scary times come I know how to handle it but does the hospital, do they have an emergency protocol for sickle cell patients? And if not why? Because of what happened to me over the course of 6 month I had so many questions. None of them a doctor could answer so I took it on myself to create a silver lining.

Well if you think it's such then I'm into that too. But the suffering I went though I want none of my brothers and sister to go through that, I was 26 worth of life prepared for that and this. I'm okay on all fronts, I would love the assistance in getting the better treatment and better education.

Count the clock
Six Hours of Pain

People say time heals all wounds, with me it doesn't, my condition is serious like a stroke with time it worsens. There's no way you can survive in time without cursing the devil out the pain makes mea scream and shout out loud at anyone who acts like they're trying to let him win, pain packed with turmoil stabbing my gut like I'm in hell paying for my sins.

So when someone is out here treating me like a nitty or fiend I really don't like it, I can only stand there take it conserve my energy before shit gets gritty.

And in that time before my body and the pain meet its killer it must be one hell of a thrill for the on looker. They must revel look at him paying for what he's done, yes because they're obviously he devil keeping my relief out of reach wanting me to jump through all their hops having fun.

Listen to me this pain isn't a fucking joke it's a serial killer waiting for bodies to lose the will to fight and day by day it molests you touches you where you don't want it can't live can't act can't play without pondering on it. It's too slick see a real warrior can feint bluff and wear the mask real well but if they told you about their true pain how much they're going through hell you wouldn't let them wait in A&E crying from Sickle Cell.

I remember well the day I went through hell I never want to feel that again the way I was treated the way I was pricked the way the doctor looked at me like I was a kid chatting shit. I came with GP note and pre established conditions but the doctors wanted to double check, first my blood then the internet? Stupid fucking idiot I remember them huddling around trying to understand what to do, their whole demeanor was making me uncomfortable. I was really writhing there muscles tensing up keeping a strong face not trying to press my luck with this serial killer waiting for me to slip up get exasperated then dehydrated every time I say I escape death there's no saying I exaggerated. I woke up -7am - IN PAIN, Walked to the GP IN PAIN, Waited at the entrance IN PAIN, Lined up IN PAIN, Got an emergency appointment IN PAIN, Waited in patience IN PAIN, Finally Spoke to my GP IN PAIN, Struggled to talk IN PAIN, Got my prescription, okay let's get these forms filled in and get a hospital note to boot.

So I can move forward; I'm in Crisis, it's not averted. Yet 20mins for the drugs but I'm still IN PAIN but if I go to the hospital with this Manila envelope they'll treat me properly I bet IN PAIN I soldier to the hospital two stops away all well is all good I made it here safe. IN PAIN but still nothing's gone wrong yet. Handed her the envelope from my GP I bet she knows what it's about I'm in a rush better get seen to quick before my time is out. My name is called YES still going right I'm IN PAIN but I bet they'll treat me right. Yes I'm here I have sickle cell, how did she ask me how do you know well

I lived with crisis for 20+ years you know. Blood pressures okay I understand that no fever CHECK yeah I passed that, I'm still IN PAIN here though, so why are you looking at me like I'm fricking a weirdo I'm sitting over here feeling like a cripple you know but I'm still in public poker face strong what the fuck you think this is here they come to take my blood to find out what the cause for my condition is how am I waiting IN PAIN for bloods IN PAIN to test if I have sickle cell IN PAIN the outpatient is testing my patience IN VEIN waiting for the doctor bet he knows what's what so I can get my prescription instead of freezing up my - - back IN PAIN I need to get away o this doctor dot care bro, why's he checking my lungs I'm starting to fear bro. Anxiety is growing I'm IN DEEP PAIN, I can't ask for drugs any more than I have without looking insane while they look on google for my prognosis I listen in terror trying to focus stay conscious and keep myself together because if I fall asleep they'll fuck up my treatment thinking I'm better,

Here you say 'falling asleep is good right you need a little rest' FUCK no before I wake up in 2hours with the Sickle Cell boring at my neck and my back ahhh shit my back I'm not ready to not walk again I better stay up.

So I wait IN PAIN, they search IN VEIN, "you better stay in the hospital to get more drugs they said" ARE YOU INSANE this isn't that type of trip did you read my GP letter ? I knew some shit like this would happen I have to stay focus I have to stay alert, oh my god the oxynorm is kicking in I'm starting to slur.

I think to myself why do I have to tango with these fucking dummies, why didn't doctor Howard pick up call back and done this now I'm in A&E IN PAIN I'm about ready to jump ship fall asleep head to the other side. No fucking way I said it before that shit is suicide.

Listen here sir I SAID IN PAIN this should have been handled earlier what's the hold up you guys have exasperated my condition left me in the cold up in the outpatient kick me out a room. When I came here for a prescription so I can deal with this at home in my room. What's with the hold up, remember I'm IN PAIN I watch them google my shit but I know he's a doctor and he's fucking vein so his hubris won't let him admit he in the wrong played up can't believe he fucked up. Give me my prescription so I can get out of here I'm IN fucking PAIN I've been here for too long I can take this pressure.

My word that was a long story and here's the end of the letter, I had no idea people wanted to treat me like a pauper. No way if I say I'm IN PAIN you better believe it wrap up what your doing and handle it quick. That's the only treatment, there is outlast the pain before it out does you that's the secret

Melancholy Maelstrom

8

It takes me a long time every time to get through that poem, not because of the length but from the pain I know it comes from that was very real pain, so much in fact. I had no idea what to do with myself during that time and all I could do eventually is write away the pain.

I have spent so many days writing now, there is something fulfilling about getting all of that pain out of my system that lifted my spirits but when I read that all the time I just want to cry and skim through it put the poem away and focus on something else, that is what made me know I have to do this because I know running away would do nothing so I leaned in, leaned all the way in and now you're not just getting some of my art you're getting this book.

I love writing essays and periodicals I do them all the time but these poems have a different essence in them I don't know what it is but I feel it. It is truly not in my spirit to write anything so personal but I had at it anyway and what I gain is a slight peace of mind. It really has allowed me to do so much more because if I can be this open with myself and make it out the other side I feel real strength to go after anything I want.

Gods Die/ No Peace of mind

On God I don't want to die tonight

They said God it ain't right, god it ain't right. They said God you strong -

But what's good, when a god dies in the middle of the night? What's good about a God that dies without a fight now all they can do is bow and pray that their blood is part of God tonight.

What's four hours to a little peace of mind what's four hours to a man that doesn't want to die tonight.

They're not gonna pray that it ain't right they're not gonna pray and say 'but he looked alright' ... he was hop skipping as singing throughout the night - a man that fights - my man that's right.

My god what's four hours to a man that doesn't wanna die tonight. - He looked left he looked right - swerve skid to the right - it moved at a speed that night - came from the left and landed on the right - prayed that he never died that night. He thought they kept it 100 plus 20 body was doing too much that night. - Whoop whoop - the coroner said he was a close call

alright.

My chest heavy clothes smelly - flooded in sweat flip the pillow - the night, ain't done yet.

Continuous gambles with God or the chemicals to give-me- one more night. Chemistry flowing intensity humming, I have the shakes like I was said to vibrate

The doctor said he's alright I said nah I felt this before there's no shooters that can get rid of this blow him up see a rainbow, spark up. Last thoughts this should do it - won't kill me give me peace of mind though I don't want drugs bro - I just want peace of mind, where's my keeper I got no peace of mind yo -. Why'd you leave me why'd you leave me? I don't feel well it's like my chest is blinking - *tap tap* see it's heavy - breath gulp can't feel myself any more all I felt was my lung it's not strong. I SWEAR THERE'S SOMETHING WRONG

Imagine wishing something wrong with me so there ain't no wasted time

I hope nothing wrong with me I just want peace of mind.

9

In me working through all this pain I knew there was something there. As an artist I can't estimate or quantify it, I can only write - when you feel the type of pain I feel, during all those times you're telling your body to do something it could do perfectly yesterday and feel so much pain today, during those time when I fight over and over. I feel.

No matter the pain *I feel* and all these thoughts and emotions that come with it and the extremities of these emotions are nothing short of tumultuous. All this pain has had to be expressed some-how, by pen via writing, or drawing or vocally. There are no other actions to take I call myself a consummate artist and live it.

I write to dedicate this piece of work to a time that doesn't need to be forgotten but one that is stamped; and all the way through this collection of works is dedicated to all the times I've been in pain and stayed quiet or couldn't explain, those time would work through it as soon as I got some feeling back or the times I pushed it to the back and out of my mind this is me looking into the eye of the eye of the demon and saying its not going to defeat me.

After all this the decision has to be made on what to do after it is expressed io choose to let go of what is there, end of the day I am a man I feel and create, either from the ether or the deep dark space within that was cultured to express freely all that was there,

I cant pus any of this down or away, it would defeat the purpose of the feeling. I was born a man and bred a fixer my consummate nature is constantly judging introspectively on what is good for the whole and the answer is always to let it go.

Let it go

The way my pain was set up it wasn't built for sharing. Not with the mind I had before, shit. Before I really wanted to - not die - I Couldn't shed a tear how upsetting, is that?

A grown man can't cry when he's supposed, to unless the pain I was suffering. Was overbearing the dam - the only thing to bust my pressure valve. Now I let the water works fly like a grown man, I tell you how.

The women I would speak to would share with me what would make their tears stream like a cold March winter, before Easter's done the emotion rears it's head like a groundhog tell em winters gone - spring is here, - spring is here. - All of my fear and despair it wasn't worth holding in treating my spirit like a ship but this ones not worth sinking, so you got to let it go - let that water out. Let yourself know you best, now you know what your feeling. - What your emotions are about. The drought is over the headaches are gone from

the rehydration of the soil in my mind. New nourishment. A
flower is born

10

As I think and write I feel myself understanding the torment that had fallen over me and I'm overcome with a bevy of emotions that I know I have to let go, I used to feel so wretched with all the things that happened but without letting this past go I know I can't moved forward; that's how these pieces become an exorcism of sorts where what I am doing and who I am is so far removed from this pain but there's a continual understanding that its not that far off.

Writing these, knowing the hope I represent for one person to keep going this is the poetic how I done it, nothing about my journey has been pretty, its really the continual effort of looking past the pain and creating more things to look forward to, architecting a future and creating spaces in time to look forward to because that's the only thing I can do, so I create share and let go.

Damilare Yusuff

Acknowledgements

I have spent so much time not convinced that my words aren't worth much, as I have told in this book there are so much value in sharing. Its made me more complete and this is a monumental shift in how I see not only my words but artistry. That being said I want to say thank you to all the people that encouraged me to do it from the Doctors that boxed me in a corner to the creative friends and artist throughout the years who told me my gift was real and pushed me to use it. A special thank you

To the artists who were there prior to the inception and gave me the nudge I needed Thank you. Those people knew I could do it so I just did it and that's how it goes sometimes. And again I want to thank you all for reading my work and getting to this stage. It's so greatly appreciated and I do hope you will all be here on the journey that transpires henceforth, this is only the beginning.

Damilare Yusuff

Melancholy Maelstrom

DAMILARE

Damilare Yusuff

Thank you for reading!

Please post a review on Amazon to let me know what you think.

Amazon reviews are integral to the success of all writers alike, if you leave one I would be extremely grateful for the time you take to support me. Please share your review on social media with the hashtag #MelancholyMaelstrom as to support new readers too.

DON'T FORGET TO
VISIT THE WEBSITE

FOR MUCH MORE ARTICLES, ESSAYS & BODIES OF WORK,
WHERE YOU CAN BE THE FIRST TO KNOW WHAT'S NEW
AND WHAT'S NEXT WITH THE AUTHOR

NYTYPICAL.NET

About the Author

Damilare spent 8 years in art and design school after a long time trying to define what it means to be as an artist. Through all this time he would writ and create stories partly from lucid dreams and mostly in part pulling from a space he calls the infinite substance where he draws from and is told all ideas originate. With that in mind his purpose is to create worlds living in, unfortunately with his condition at play he discovered that his reality is bleak and now more than writing stories he seeks to change the world around him by educating and his productions. Damilare writes with the ideal to create a better landscape for under served and disenfranchised people. Starting with this book and his website nytypical.net

Connect with Damilare

Facebook	nytypical
Instagram	nytypical
Twitter:	nytypical
Website:	nytypical.net

www.ingramcontent.com/pod-product-compliance
Lightning Source LLC
Chambersburg PA
CBHW061051050726
47592CB00004B/1638